Other books in this series:
A Feast of After Dinner Jokes   A Bouquet of Wedding Jokes
A Portfolio of Business Jokes   A Spread of Over 40s Jokes
A Round of Golf Jokes   A Binge of Diet Jokes
A Romp of Naughty Jokes   A Knockout of Sports Jokes

Published in the USA in 1993 by Exley Giftbooks
Published in Great Britain in 1993 by Exley Publications Ltd
Second printing 1994

Cartoons © Bill Stott 1993
Copyright © Helen Exley 1993
ISBN 1-85015-402-3

Series Editor: Helen Exley.
Editor: Elizabeth Cotton

The publishers gratefully acknowledge permission to reprint copyright material. They would
be pleased to hear from any copyright holders not here acknowledged.
Extracts from *Jokes, Quotes and One-Liners* by Herbert V. Prochnow and Herbert V. Prochnow
Jr, reprinted by permission of Harper Collins; extracts from *Murphy's Law* and *Murphy's Law
Bk II* © 1977 & 1980 by Arthur Bloch, reprinted by permission Methuen London; extracts
from *Henry Youngman's Book of Jokes* by Henny Youngman reprinted by permission of the
Carol Publishing Group; extracts from *The Official Rules* by Paul Dixon, reprinted by
permission of Arrow Books; extract from *The Wit's Dictionary* by Colin Bowles and *The
World's Best Motoring Jokes* by Edward Phillips, reprinted by kind permission of Angus and
Robertson (a division of Harper Collins Publishing Ltd.); extracts from *The Return of Heroic
Failures* by Stephen Pile, reprinted by permission of Rogers, Coleridge & White Ltd.; extracts
from *". . . And Finally"* by Martyn Lewis reproduced by permission of Hutchinson.

Cover designed by Pinpoint Design Company
Typeset by Delta, Watford. Printed at Oriental Press, UAE

Exley Publications Ltd, 16 Chalk Hill, Watford, Herts WD1 4BN, United Kingdom.
Exley Giftbooks, 232 Madison Avenue, Suite 1206, NY 10016, USA.

—A TANKFUL OF—
MOTORING
• J O K E S •

Cartoons by Bill Stott

≣EXLEY
NEW YORK • WATFORD, UK

CAR CRAZY

"How did you win that new car, John?"

"Oh, I just saved the tops of corn flake packets until I earned it. Good car too - plenty of room to sleep in."

"Sleep in?"

"Sure, the house is full of corn flakes."

HERBERT V. PROCHNOW & HERBERT V. PROCHNOW JR.

*

"Mr. Sims, an eccentric millionaire who took me on a trip to Europe, on arriving in Paris hired three cars – one upholstered in grey, to go with a grey suit, a second in blue, to go with a blue suit, and a third in brown, for a brown suit. The driver of each car was to be appropriately clad. Each morning the three cars would come to the hotel to await his pleasure. Sims would make his choice according to which suit his whim had indicated for that day. If he changed at noon we would shift cars."

DR. WILLIAM E. AUGHINBAUGH, from I Swear by Apollo

*

"Americans are broad-minded . . . They'll accept the fact that a person can be an alcoholic, a dope fiend, a wife beater, and even a newspaper man, but if a man doesn't drive, there's something wrong with him."
ART BUCHWALD

*

"WOULD I STILL LOVE YOU IF YOU DROVE A PANEL VAN? HMM - PULL OVER AND GIVE ME TEN MINUTES TO THINK ABOUT THAT ONE."

BREAKDOWN

"Driving out in the country, a motorist came across a car pulled in at the side of the road with a puncture. By the side of the car stood a woman looking very distressed. Feeling gallant the motorist stopped and offered to help. He changed the wheel and was letting the jack down, when the woman said, 'Please let it down gently - my husband is sleeping in the back.'"

PETER GRAY

"A motorist whose car had broken down on a deserted country road was staring helplessly into the engine when, to her amazement, a cow wandered up. She stood beside the motorist, also staring into the engine. Then chewing casually she said, 'It's your carburettor that's the problem.'

The motorist was so surprised that she ran off down the road, until she came to a farmer leaning over a gate. Breathlessly, she told him the amazing story of the speaking cow.

'Was she a brown cow with a silver cow bell?'

'Yes! Yes!' replied the motorist excitedly.

'Well, I wouldn't take any notice. That's Bella, and she don't know a darned thing about cars.'"

C.M.

Sharing The Road

Anthea's Rules of Driving Courtesy:

If you allow someone to get in front of you, either:

a) the car in front will be the last one over a railroad crossing, and you will be stuck waiting for a long, slow-moving train; or

b) you both will have the same destination, and the other car will get the last parking space.

ARTHUR BLOCH, from *Murphy's Law*

∗

"One rainy morning a young woman driver stalled her car at a traffic light. She was having difficulty starting up her damp engine and her efforts weren't helped by the impatient driver behind her who kept honking his horn rudely.

After some more fumbling with her reluctant engine, the young woman got out and walked up to the car behind. 'I'm terribly sorry,' she said politely, 'I seem to be having a problem starting my car. If you'd be so kind as to come and have a look at it for me, I'll stay here and lean on your horn.'"

M.C.G.

"I DON'T KNOW - YOU CAN'T EVEN WOLF WHISTLE AND
SHOUT 'I WOULDN'T MIND SOME OF THAT' THESE DAYS
WITHOUT GETTING ABUSE!"

"I THOUGHT I HEARD A BUMP WHEN WE PULLED UP - YOU'VE

RUN OVER THE WRETCHED CHAP'S BEETLE!"

WATCH OUT BEHIND!

"Cursed is he that does not know the width
of his car."

CHRISTOPHER DRIVER

*

A tree (n.): Something that stands in the same
place for a hundred years and then suddenly jumps
out behind a reversing car.

ANON

*

Accused: "I was certainly not driving at 60 miles
an hour in a built-up area! I wasn't doing more than
40 miles an hour, in fact it was nearer 30. Now I
come to think about it, I'd slowed down to 20 at the
time and..."

Judge: "Hold on a minute! You'd better stop
before you back into someone!"

*

Speed Freaks

"The automobile of tomorrow will be faster than sound. You'll be in hospital before you start the motor."

HENNY YOUNGMAN

"LEFT YOU STANDING AT THE LIGHTS, EH SONNY?"

"SOME ACCELERATION, HUH?"

The young man pulled up and grinned when the policewoman told him sternly that he had been doing over eighty.

"Isn't that great!" he exclaimed. "And I'm only just learning to drive!"

*

Some people drive as if they were anxious to get all their accidents over and done with quickly.

*

OFF TO THE COUNTRY!

August is the month when motorists load up their cars with the mother-in-law, the kids, the dog, the budgie, a dozen carrier bags, three picnic baskets, two radios and then head off to the country to "get away from it all".

*

Driving over a mountain pass a lady motorist narrowly missed a head-on collision when another car came swerving around a tight corner. As the two cars passed, a large man in a peaked cap stuck his head out of the window and shouted, "Cow!". Angered by his apparent rudeness, the lady wound down her own window and yelled, "Pig!".

She rounded the corner and drove smack bang into a cow.

*

"Having a four-wheel drive just means you get stuck in more inaccessible places."

M.C.G.

*

"REMEMBER YOUR MOTHER GETTING OUT TO ADMIRE THE VIEW
A FEW MILES BACK? DID SHE GET BACK IN?"

"THERE'S THE PROBLEM - A HIBERNATING DIAMOND-BACK
RATTLESNAKE STUCK IN THE AIR CLEANER - IT'S ALWAYS
HAPPENING ON THESE MK IIIS ...."

Beware Of The Mechanic

Three elderly men were sitting at the bar drinking. "What's the most frightening sound you can think of?" one asked.

"The howl of a wolf in a dark forest."

"Heavy footsteps behind you in a deserted alley."

"They're nothing," said the oldest and wisest. "The most fearful noise known to man is the long, low whistle coming from a mechanic underneath your car."

Campbell's Laws of Automotive Repair:

1. If you can get to the faulty part, you don't have the tool to get it off.

2. If you can get the part off, the parts house will have it back-ordered.

3. If it's in stock, it didn't need replacing in the first place.

ARTHUR BLOCH, from *Murphy's Law*

RULES OF THE ROAD

Barrett's Laws of Driving:

1) You can get anywhere in ten minutes if you go fast enough.

2) Speed bumps are of negligible effect when the vehicle exceeds triple the desired restraining speed.

3) The vehicle in front of you is travelling slower than you are.

4) This lane ends in 500 feet.

JOHN L. SHELDON, from *The Official Rules*

*

Quigley's Law:

A car and a truck approaching each other on an otherwise deserted road will meet at the narrow bridge.

Law of Life's Highway:

If everything is coming your way, you're in the wrong lane.

ARTHUR BLOCH, from *Murphy's Law*

*

"I DON'T CARE IF IT IS THE ONLY SPACE - I AM NOT GETTING OUT THROUGH THE SUN ROOF!"

No Parking

"Things are rough. People are worried. I saw a man lying in the gutter the other day. I walked up and said, 'Are you sick? Can I help you?'

He said, 'No, I found a parking space, I sent my wife out to buy a car.'"

HENNY YOUNGMAN, from *Henry Youngman's Book of Jokes*

street (n.) a broad, flat surface used for the storage of "no parking" signs.

from *The Wall Street Journal*

*

Benson's Corollary of Inverse Distances:

The farther away from the entrance of the market (theater, or any other given location) that you have to park, the closer the space vacated by the car that pulls away as you walk up to the door.

JUDITH DEMILLE BERSON, from *The Official Rules*

*

GOING NOWHERE SLOWLY

A Texan on vacation in Scotland was bragging about the size of his ranch to a Scottish farmer. "I can get into my car at 5.30 in the morning and drive all day till it gets dark, and I still won't have reached half-way across my property."

"Och, yes," nodded the farmer sympathetically. "I had a car like that once."

"I used to own a car specially designed for five people: one had to drive while the other four pushed."

J.K.C.

*

"My car's so old it doesn't even have a speedometer."

"How do you tell how fast you're going?"

"Easy. At 20 mph, the wheels rattle, at 30 mph the doors rattle. And if I go any faster I rattle."

*

"The last time I took the car for a road test, they warned me that the only parts of it which could be considered road worthy were the sun-visor and one ashtray."

DENIS NORDEN

automobile (n.) a guided missile.

ANON

careful driver: one who looks in both directions when he passes a red light.

RALPH MARTERIE

freeway (n.) a place where drivers under 25 do over 90 and drivers over 90 do under 25.

ANON

mechanic (n.) a person who picks your pocket from underneath your car.

COLIN BOWLES, from *The Wit's Dictionary*

model driver (n.) someone who just saw the car ahead of her get a traffic ticket.

ANON

rush hour: that hour when the traffic is almost at a standstill.

J.B. MORTON

"The two biggest features on the new cars are airbrakes and unbreakable windshields. You can get up to 100 miles an hour and stop on a dime. Then you press this special button and a putty knife scrapes you off the windshield!"

HENNY YOUNGMAN, from *Henny Youngman's Book of Jokes*

*

"I never cease to be amazed at the advances of technology. Have you noticed if you stop at traffic lights and they turn green, that the horn of the car behind is immediately activated?"

PETER GRAY

*

They've invented this new feature for cars. If you want to turn left you press a button and a sign starts flashing saying, "I'm turning left." If you want to turn right you press a button and a sign starts flashing saying, "I'm turning right." There's a special button for kids learning to drive. It says, "I don't know what I'm going to do next."

*

"These days the motorist reigns supreme and it's the poor old pedestrian who is always in the wrong. Last week a man was hit by a car and knocked thirty feet in the air. He was arrested for leaving the scene of the accident."

EDWARD PHILLIPS, from *The World's Best Motoring Jokes*

"All things come to she who crosses the street against the red light."

M.C.G.

*

"A girl stood on the side of the road trying to cross. The stream of traffic was never ending, and not wishing to risk her life, she was about to give up when she saw another pedestrian on the other side.

'Hey!' she called, 'how did you get over there?'

The other woman turned and shouted back, 'I was born here!'"

PETER GRAY

*

"A witness giving evidence in court concerning a traffic accident was asked by the magistrate what, in his opinion, was the cause of the collision. 'As far as I could see,' he replied, 'both drivers seemed to be chasing the same pedestrian.'"

EDWARD PHILLIPS, from The World's Best Motoring Jokes

*

READING THE SIGNS

Road sign next to a river:

    When this sign is underwater the road is impassable.

*

Street sign: For that run-down feeling why not try jay-walking?

On an ancient car: I bought this at an auction - what's your excuse?

This car may be old - but it's in front of you and it's paid for!

0 - 60 in 15 minutes.

*

Money, Money, Money

"I passed a car dealer's shop. I looked in the window and I saw the most beautiful cars. And a fellow came out and said, 'Come on in, they're bigger than ever and they last a lifetime!' He was talking about the payments."

CORBETT MONICA

*

"Kim had always dreamt of owning her own car, and when she saw an advert for a Corvette she just couldn't resist. The car was all she'd ever wanted, but there was a problem – the money. Before long she fell behind with the monthly payments. Sick with worry she called into her bank manager's office for some advice.

'Well, it's quite simple,' he said, 'either you give up the car or quit eating.'

After five minutes Kim still hadn't said a word.

'What's the problem?' her bank manager asked.

'I'm still thinking,' came the miserable reply. 'I'm still thinking.'"

E.P.R.

"I bought myself a new car and the first thing I done was grease it all over – so the finance company can't get a hold of it."

ROD BRASFIELD

"FORTY TO THE GALLON? MILES OR YARDS?"

"WHAT'S MEXICAN FOR TOP HOSE?"

True Story

"Far too many Sunday drivers are happy to pootle around for a weekend hour or two following dull itineraries. Only Mr. Joseph Strophel of Dunedin in Georgia has transformed this activity into the adventure of a lifetime.

Announcing that he was going out for a short drive in September 1987, Mr. Strophel took a wrong turning and got happily lost in the dense network of twisting backroads. Three days later he was the subject of a nationwide search with regular bulletins on every radio station.

Seven days later Ms. Kathleen Stubblefield passed his car as far away as Indiana. She chased after him and flagged him down. Relaxing at the Stubblefield residence in Blairsville, Mr. Strophel said he had travelled 1,700 miles in the past week. It appears that he had motored extensively in several states including Tennessee, Indiana and Kentucky."

STEPHEN PILE, from *The Return of Heroic Failures*

*

"NO - IT'S AS DEAD AS A DODO. DID YOU FEEL A BUMP JUST
BEFORE WE STOPPED?"

REPAIRS

Hartman's Automotive Laws:

   1) Nothing minor ever happens to a car at the
weekend.

   2) Nothing minor ever happens to a car on a trip.

   3) Nothing minor ever happens to a car.

CHARLES D. HARTMAN, from The Official Rules

*

"The new trainee at the garage arrived with all his
tools, eager to be let loose on a car.

The boss looked at him solemnly.

'First things first, lad. You have to master the
basics. Now then, open the bonnet. Stare. Lean
forward. Stare. Sigh. Now say after me: Oh dear, oh
dear, oh dear.'"

PAM BROWN

*

Car mechanic to motorist:

   "The cost of repairs will be twenty for parts, plus
twelve for the work, plus a fee of ten for not
overcharging you."

<u>CRUNCH!</u>

It is a well known fact that the part of the car that causes the most accidents is the nut that holds the wheel.

The driver of a brand new car stopped at a road junction and was driven into by the car behind. The damage was minimal, so she just glared at the offender and drove on. At the next set of traffic lights

the same thing happened. After the third collision the guilty driver got out of his car and came over ready to swap insurance details.

"Never mind that," said the woman. "Just give me a five-minute head start."

*

"Driving-school instructor to befuddled pupil: 'You still have a few minutes of your lesson left, shall I show you how to fill in the accident forms?'"

BENNET CERF

*

Learning To Drive

"I've been teaching my young nephew how to drive. He's invented something completely new called an O-turn. He says it can be used when you're making a U-turn and you change your mind."

J. E. BROWN

*

"In the early 1970s Mrs. Helen Ireland of Auburn in California failed her driving test in the first second.

She got into the car, said 'Good morning' to the tester and started the engine. However, she mistook the accelerator for the clutch and shot straight through the wall of the Driving Test Centre."

STEPHEN PILE, from The Return of Heroic Failures

Grandpa Charnock's Law:

You never really learn to swear until you learn to drive.

ARTHUR BLOCH, from Murphy's Law Bk II

"ON THIS VEHICLE, MR. BENSTOCK, ONLY THE GEARS ARE AUTOMATIC. IT STILL REQUIRES MANUAL STEERING."

BEATEN BY TECHNOLOGY

"On a cold and frosty winter morning, a man heard his wife trying, unsuccessfully, to start the car. Again and again she tried to get the engine turning, but it just wouldn't catch. Eventually he went out to the garage.

'Didn't you try choking it?' he asked.

'No,' his wife replied through gritted teeth, 'but I darn well felt like it.'"

PETER GRAY

"A woman who seemed to be recovering well from an operation was driven by her mother to the doctor's surgery for a check-up. The patient opened the door, started to get out, and suddenly fell back against the seat. 'Not as strong as I thought,' she gasped. 'You'd better help me.'

Alarmed, her mother rushed round to the other side of the car. 'Easy, now,' she pleaded. 'Let's try it together.'

It wasn't until the third try that they thought of unfastening the seat belt."

J.C.M.

✳

"Grandma," asked the inquisitive four-year-old,
"what happens when a car is too old to run any more?"
"Someone sells it to your grandfather."

"IT'S JUST THE CAR FOR YOU, SIR - UNREMARKABLE,

SIMPLE, QUIET...."

"ACTUALLY, I COULDN'T GIVE A DAMN WHAT PRICE IT IS - HAS IT GOT <u>GRUNT</u>?"

"My new car turned out to have defective brakes. I took it back to the dealer and said, 'Forget about standing behind the car - I want you to stand in front of it.'"

M.C.G.

*

Speaking of buying used cars... remember it's hard to drive a bargain...

*

Policeman: "Why didn't you stop when I shouted to you?"

Motorist: "I'm sorry, officer, I didn't realize it was a policeman yelling, I thought it was someone I'd run over."

*

"HOW DARE YOU? COMING STRAIGHT AT ME FLASHING YOUR LIGHTS - I'LL HAVE YOU KNOW I'M A PERSONAL FRIEND OF THE POLICE CHIEF!"

"Didn't you realize it was a one-way street? Didn't you see the arrows?"

"Arrows? I didn't even see the Indians."

*

Be warned... 80% of people consider themselves to be above average drivers.

*

"THIS IS A ONE-WAY STREET, SIR."

"THIS SHOULD BE GOOD...."

Ouch!

"Mrs. Baker finished her shopping and was about to start her journey home when she found that someone had driven into her car which she had parked in a busy street. The damage was considerable, headlights were smashed and the front fender was badly dented. Tucked under her windscreen wiper was a note that read, "I reversed into your car as I was trying to park. There were lots of witnesses so I thought I'd better leave a note. I bet they all thought I was leaving my name and address so you could get in touch with me."

PAM BROWN

*

The Sunday school teacher was telling her class of six-year-olds how Lot's wife turned into a pillar of salt, when one small girl chimed in, "My mother looked back once while she was driving, and she turned into a telegraph pole."

*

"Is it true you've bought a Beetle? Whatever do you want a little car like that for?"

"My chauffeur needs something to stand on while he washes the limo."

"THE PATTERSONS ARE HERE - IN THEIR NEW CONVERTIBLE..."

"The sports-car owner was giving a friend his first ride in one of the low-slung models. The friend appeared to be puzzled, so the driver asked what was wrong.

'I can't figure it out. What's that long wall we're passing.'

'That's no wall,' snapped the driver, 'it's the curb.'"

HERBERT V. PROCHNOW & HERBERT V. PROCHNOW Jr.

*

"A wealthy Australian sheep-farmer walked into a car showroom and bought a brand-new Rolls-Royce. After paying cash, he said, 'An' I want a glass partition fitted between the drivin' seat and the back.'

'I'm afraid we don't fit those any more,' said the salesman. 'There's no call for them.'

'Look, sport,' said the Australian, 'when I'm drivin' this car back home in New South Wales, I don't want the flamin' sheep lickin' the back of me neck!'"

EDWARD PHILLIPS, from *The World's Best Motoring Jokes*

*

MANIACS!

"Shutting her eyes and uttering a short prayer, the lady tourist wondered if she'd live to tell the tale of her first journey in a New York cab. The cab driver sped through the crowded streets, weaving in and out of other traffic, pedestrians leapt out of the way to avoid being crashed into. She looked ahead and saw a lorry overtaking in a narrow street. Instead of slowing down, the cab accelerated and missed a head-on collision by inches.

'Are you trying to get us both killed?' she screamed.

'Relax, lady,' came the reply. 'Do what I do - close your eyes.'"

E.H.C.

*

"And then I saw him driving straight towards me."

"Why didn't you pull over and give him half the road?"

"Well, I was going to just as soon as I'd figured out which half he wanted."

*

"Always try to drive so that your license will expire before you do."

C.C.H.

*

"THE ELECTRIC CAR: ITS COMPACT TURNING CIRCLE MATCHED ONLY BY THE SIZE OF ITS DRIVER'S BRAIN."

"Never lend your car to anyone to whom you have given birth."

ERMA BOMBECK

＊

A motorcycle policeman was out patrolling a busy stretch of highway. He was horrified to see a young man driving at high speed, holding the steering wheel between his knees and playing a guitar. He signalled to him to pull over and asked angrily, "Don't you know you're endangering the lives of hundreds of people?"

"'Fraid I don't sir" the youth replied, "but if you hum it I'll try and strum along."

＊

Once upon a time, when a young man took the keys to the garage he would come out with the lawn mower.

＊

"I KNOW YOU'RE VERY SAFETY CONSCIOUS, BUT BRIAN IS 15 - COULDN'T HE JUST USE ORDINARY REAR SEAT BELTS NOW?"

"THIS GIANT CHICKEN YOU SWERVED TO AVOID - EXACTLY

HOW TALL WAS IT?"

EXCUSES, EXCUSES

From a letter written to an insurance company:

"I collided with a stationary lorry coming the other way."

*

Policeman: "What's the idea of weaving about all over the road like that?"

Motorist: "I'm sorry, Officer, I've just washed my car and I can't do a thing with it."

EDWARD PHILLIPS, from The World's Best Motoring Jokes

*

"A 23-year-old Swede was driving a vanload of mice to a Gothenburg hospital for use in experiments when he skidded off the road. He told the court that the breath of hundreds of mice fogged the windscreen so badly that he had to bend down to pick up a cloth to wipe it clear - and that was when he landed up in the ditch. The court wasn't entirely convinced."

MARTYN LEWIS, from And Finally

*

FAMOUS LAST WORDS

I know this road like the back of my hand...

When that light shows there's still *plenty* of gas left...

Don't panic! It's my right of way...

There's plenty of space – you could park a tank there...

"YOU HEAR A FUNNY NOISE THEN?"

With these brakes I could stop on a dime...

Oooh! Look at that beautiful view!

I've only had one. Besides *I* can hold my drink...

*